IS COMMERCIAL REAL ESTATE FOR YOU?

Greg Biggs

A GUIDE TO CAREERS IN ONE OF THE
WORLD'S MOST DYNAMIC, REWARDING,
AND LUCRATIVE PROFESSIONS

ISBN: 978-1-54390-706-3 (print)
ISBN: 978-1-54390-707-0 (ebook)

CONTENTS

Forward

by Roger T. Staubach

When I started my career in commercial real estate in the 1970s, my focus was on supporting my wife and our three children. Player salaries in the NFL were not what they are today and if something happened to me, I wanted to make sure my family was taken care of.

I was very fortunate to learn from the best. Henry S. Miller, Jr., a commercial real estate legend and leader, took me under his wing and taught me the lay of the land during my off-seasons. Working with him was the beginning of my life in commercial real estate. He set a great example. The best advice I got in the business was from him. He preached a message of integrity and how making the right decisions now will affect the future.

Henry was a great mentor and friend. He gave his time and guidance, providing the foundation for my career in commercial real estate. That is something I will always be grateful for.

Having the right people in the right places is important, but getting the right people in the right places working together is critical to the long-term success for our clients and ourselves. This is something

I instilled in the Staubach Company when we started in 1977 and became a part of JLL in 2008. It's a part of our culture.

Our industry is continuously evolving, but the pillars remain the same. This book will provide you the overview of commercial real estate and the opportunities our industry holds within it.

Our guys have heard me say it a million times – "You want to win the business. You want to do it right. The rewards follow."

The same applies here. You want to win the business. You need to know the business. The rewards will follow.

Author's Note

WHY THIS BOOK

As you gain tenure in your career, you may be asked by friends, colleagues, or company leaders to meet with others – often times young people just out of college – who are interested in getting into your business. My mentor, Tom Kelly - one of the best salesmen I've ever met - taught me that providing career guidance is a great way to give back to our industry.

This certainly seems to be true. But in meeting with young people who want to get into commercial real estate, there seems to be a big disconnect between perception and reality. They'll say, "I want to get into the commercial real estate business". But when asked what field they wanted to pursue, a majority of the time – and understandably so - they don't know what field they're interested in or know enough about the industry to have a preference.

Colleagues and peers have shared similar experiences. So after looking for a book that could be recommended to those interested in a commercial real estate career – one that would break down the various fields and the roles in the industry, it seems that there are very few resources to recommend.

This book intends to fill that void.

Hopefully this book will help you better understand the commercial real estate business from a high level – and guide you to a discipline that sparks your interests and suits your strengths, ensuring long-term success!

CHAPTER I

GETTING STARTED

Commercial real estate is a dynamic industry that's rich with opportunity. It's also unique, because in one way or another, it touches every type of business. Name a company, and there will be some sort of commercial real estate involved.

You might say, "Wait. What about online businesses, or the cloud?" Well, the cloud doesn't exist in outer space, but on Earth in data centers. Online companies couldn't function without data centers, and many, including giants like Amazon, also require office space for programmers, marketers, and other employees, as well as warehouse space to store and distribute the products they sell.

Because it's so broad, commercial real estate can appear to be confusing. After all, there are more than 90 fields of work (not all will be covered in this book) in the industry! But once you understand the different product types and the disciplines that work within them, you'll see it's not complicated at all.

Narrowing the Field

When pursuing a career in commercial real estate, it's important to narrow your field of interest as soon as possible. You'll have a head start if you can build your college coursework around the discipline. And as you interview with prospective employers, you'll stand out if you have a clear focus and thoughtful plan.

The product types we will discuss in this book are: land, office, industrial, data centers, retail, hospitality, healthcare and multifamily. (Another, mixed-use, refers to a combination of one or more product types.)

The various disciplines we'll review are: architecture, appraisal, capital markets, construction, development, leasing, investment, management, research and analytics, and tenant representation.

The following illustration may help you visualize how it all works. (The various product types are inside the globe, and the disciplines and fields that touch them are surrounding the globe.

CHAPTER 2

LAND

Many years, ago Will Rogers said something that is quoted still today: "Put your money in land because they aren't making any more of it." How true and prophetic. However, land is significantly different from other real estate product types because there is no cash flow and there is a lack of sales capability during down cycles.

Speculative Land Investing

The challenge with land investment is that there is no income or cash flow from land. It is purchased on the hope and optimism that future development will catch up to the site and make the site more valuable during the hold period or that the investor can create a development on the site that will create value increase for the land and the new development.

When buying speculative investment land, success is largely determined at the time of purchase. If the site purchased is the wrong piece at the wrong time for too much money, then the hold period is longer and profit is reduced, or eliminated, creating a loss. A land investor needs to be focused, disciplined and unemotional about the site or the development...which is easier said than done. Emotional purchases have taken down many investors.

To buy a land site and hold it for appreciation takes time and patience. Although land does not have extensive income/expense projections, there are other factors that can make an investment profitable or not. These factors include zoning, utilities, municipal desire, competition, demand, hold period, market conditions, and of course, the investment amount.

The goal with land investment is appreciation. Since land is not liquid, it is commonly thought of as risky. But with this risk comes large appreciation if the right choices are made. Historically, the appreciated value and subsequent wealth created with land is what draws its investors.

The basic idea is to evaluate land sites and determine where the development growth is headed and get in front of it. Some investors will say, "If you can see the roads, you are too late to make the best speculative buy".

What long term investors look for are land site (tracts) that are poised to take advantage of future roads, water/sewer utilities and advantageous zoning. When land investors find the convergence of these factors, an investment is made. The final question is, "If I buy it, when will I sell it?"

This is the hardest question to answer. If the right evaluation has been done but the real estate cycle has been misread, the investment will under-perform. However, if the cycle is read well, the profits will be well worth the hold period.

Cypress Waters 2011

Land Development

Development of land takes vision and capital. The below developments started out as raw land in favorable locations with the developers having a vision and master plan for the land. Although full development takes years to complete, the final product will have numerous uses that complement the projects, creating a fully master planned community that includes offices, hotels, multi-family, retail businesses and other uses that attract businesses and people.

Granite Park 2004

The appropriate purchase of a land site for the developer's concept is critical to the development's success. For the development to work financially, the fundamentals are the same as the long term investor. The site will ultimately need the appropriate zoning, the utilities to support the site and the need to be in a location that works for the development. Timing is also critical to new development. The photos below show the same development sites mid-way through the completion of the development.

Cypress Waters 2016

Granite Park 2012

Zoning is a critical piece of the development puzzle because it describes the outright and conditional uses for the land that the controlling governmental authority has approved. It may also indicate the size and demission of the land area as well as the form and scale of buildings for the property. Zoning guidelines are set in order to guide the urban growth and development. There are typically a great variety of zoning types and the types and definitions will depend in each municipality. Zoning may also include regulation of the kinds of activities which will be acceptable on particular sites within the development (such as open space, residential, agricultural, commercial or industrial). Densities at which these uses can be built (from low-density housing such as single family homes to high-density such as high-rise apartment buildings), the height of buildings, the amount of space structures may occupy, the location of a building on the lot (setbacks), the proportions of the types of space on a lot, such as how much landscaped space, impervious surface, traffic lanes, and whether or not parking is provided may also be included in the zoning.

Even though the zoning for a site may be set, it is not uncommon for investors or developers to try to get the zoning changed to a different type. Their hope is by changing the zoning, the use they want to place on the property will add more value. The process to change the zoning will vary from municipality to municipality and sometimes can take time and be a lengthy process.

To help spur development and help increase real estate values, municipalities will often create tax increment financing (TIF) districts. These are special purpose districts which allow the municipality to reinvest added tax revenue from new development back into the area where it originated. They are essentially used as a subsidy for redevelopment, infrastructure, and other community-improvement projects. Any increase in tax revenues (caused by new development and higher property values) is paid into the TIF fund to finance certain improvements. Potential improvements include but are not limited to: wider sidewalks, utility installation or improvements, public landscaping, lighting, environmental remediation, demolition and historic facades.

Land Brokers

There are brokerage professionals that focus just on land transactions. They are knowledgeable with the factors that go into the evaluation of a land site and should be able to envision how the market will evolve. In other words, they have a future vision for the land and their vision is about the future that could be created on the land. They must be knowledgeable about all of the same things the investor and developer need to know and maybe even more. A good land broker understands that a buyer or purchaser could become a long term client given the right advice and counsel about a site.

Although land investment is not thought of in the same way as income producing properties, it is not an <u>unsophisticated</u> investment. After all, all development begins with the land.

Ultimately, a well planned development will provide numerous amenities to the surrounding businesses and residence and increase significant value from tax revenue to the municipality and county of the development.

Cypress Waters Master Plan

Granite Park 2017

CHAPTER 3

OFFICE

Office buildings come in many different sizes and designs and have a number of functional uses. They can range from a small, single-story building to a towering high-rise or a corporate campus with multiple buildings and millions of square feet.

Dallas Skyline

Capital One Campus

Downtowns and other urban areas are business parks in and of themselves. "Suburban-urban" is an evolving type of development where office buildings are matched up with retail and residential space (mixed-use) to form "cities within cities."

Office buildings can be "single-tenant" (occupied by just one company) or multi-tenant (shared by many different businesses). Office buildings are also separated into different classes: Class A buildings are typically newer facilities with the latest amenities, in the best locations with covered parking that have lease rates that are the most expensive in the market; Class B buildings attract market-average rents, have fewer amenities and may have a portion but not all, of the parking covered; Class C buildings are older, have below-average lease rates with few amenities and typically surface parking. Sometimes brand-new luxury office buildings are referred to as Class AA.

Office buildings are traditionally leased by the square foot. There are three types of leases from a financial perspective for office buildings.

1. Full service leases – Leases that include the rent, the operating expenses and the electricity for the leased space. The tenant pays the landlord the total amount of all of these costs, typically monthly, based on the negotiate rate.

2. Net leases – Leases that include the rent and operating expenses but NOT the electricity. The tenant pays the rent and estimated operating expense to the landlord but is charged separately for their electrical consumption.

3. NNN Leases – Leases that are rent only and do not include the operating expenses and electricity. The tenant pays the rent to the landlord and then pays the operating expenses and electrical consumption separately.

Parking is another component that is important to users of office space. Office buildings typically provide a parking ratio for the buildings. In urban core locations the parking ratio is usually very low (1 space per 2000 square feet of space leased, referred as 1/2000 SF) versus suburban buildings that have more land and can provide more parking to the tenant (1 space per 250 square feet leased, referred as 1/250 SF).

Parking ratios and pricing may be negotiated but are typically set by market conditions. Reserved parking is traditionally more expensive than non-reserved parking, as is covered parking versus non-covered parking.

From a construction perspective, office space can be broken down into four primary facility types. Below is a breakdown of each:

High-Rise

High-rise buildings are from 25 stories tall to the world's largest building in Dubai which is 162 stories or over 2,700 feet tall, truly a skyscraper. These buildings have a larger core area, due to the multiple elevator systems needed for the number of floors in the building. These high-rise buildings are built with steel and have a much more expensive exterior glass curtain-wall system. The glass system has to be much more robust to handle the wind loads of a high-rise building. This type of construction is typically delivered in a "warm shell" condition to tenants. Warm shell means that the landlord will install the base building lobby, elevators, elevator lobbies on each floor, the restrooms on each floor and the multi-tenant corridor (hall ways) on those floors. High-rise buildings usually have only a small amount of parking associated with them, due to the cost and or lack of availability of land to accommodate the parking. In most downtown areas, mass transit is the preferred way to commute.

Bank of America Plaza under construction   *Bank of America Plaza*

Traditional Mid-Rise

Mid-rise office buildings are four to 25 stories tall and use a different construction process than tilt-wall construction. The buildings use what's called a "poured-in-place concrete, curtain wall" approach. In the following photos, you can see that each floor is poured individually, and typically takes a week to construct before the next floor can begin. The pre-cast (made at an off-site pre-cast plant) exterior walls and windows are hung floor by floor. The floor plates are more efficient because the interior core area (elevators, restrooms and mechanical and electrical rooms) requires less elevator space than a high-rise skyscraper.

Traditional mid-rise space is typically delivered in a "warm shell" condition, as described above. These buildings are usually built with structured parking, either attached to the office building or underneath the structure. Although it adds to the cost of development, mid-rise structures are frequently built on sites with structured parking and marketed to tenants who are willing to pay for that amenity.

Granite Park V under construction   *Granite Park V*

Tilt-Wall

Lower profile buildings can have a number of different names, such as R&D (research & development), flex, or value office. These facilities use "tilt-wall" construction with a flat roof. They're built by pouring the concrete for the walls of the building within a form on the floor of the building, letting them cure and raising them up in place with a crane and securing with steel poles while the walls are welded together and the roof is installed. This type of construction is often delivered to the tenants in a condition called "cold, dark shell".

Literally, the developer or landlord provides the floor, walls and roof. All MEP-mechanical (HVAC), electrical and plumbing – systems are installed by the tenant occupying the space.

Tilt-wall construction has morphed in recent years into multi-floor buildings with as many as four or five stories. Due to a lower cost of construction, these "value office" buildings are typically less expensive than traditional mid-rise office structures.

Multi-story, tilt-wall facilities can utilize covered or surface parking or a combination of the two. There are two ways to accomplish covered parking. The first approach is to build canopies. This will add to the cost of the building, but – depending on the amount of canopy spaces – not as significant a cost as structured parking. The second approach is structured (garage) parking. This may be used for projects with smaller land tracts or to accomplish higher parking density ratios or just due to the demands of the tenant. The cost of structured parking can add a significant amount to the overall cost of the building, depending on the number of levels of the garage.

Legacy Center under construction

Legacy Center

Stick-Built

Single-story buildings can be built much like a residential home. Often referred to as "stick-built", these structures are framed out of wood and often overlaid with a brick façade. These buildings are used to house small businesses or small medical practices. They utilize commercial-grade electrical and HVAC (Heating, Ventilation, and Air Conditioning) systems and typically have surface parking. These buildings are the least expensive to build, own, or lease.

As mentioned, when newly constructed, each of these office building types, are delivered and leased to tenants in "Cold Dark Shell or Warm Shell Conditions". From there, the tenant is responsible for the interior "Tenant Improvements". Most of the time, the Landlord will provide a Tenant Improvement Allowance which is often a negotiated amount. The cost of the tenant improvements will vary depending on the level of office space vs open space (typically office cube furniture) ratio and the level of finishes a company utilizes within its space. Law firm office space is significantly more expensive than a sales office finish out.

Retrofitting office space after the space has been finished out can be more expensive than the original finish out due to the fact that the next tenant to move in usually will want to make changes to the space, requiring demolition of a portion or all of the space, which adds to the cost of the tenant improvement construction.

A company's office space is critical to its success. Location decisions are no longer made only by evaluating just the per-square-foot costs. Buildings are selected today by companies to house their businesses for their accessibility to sufficient parking or mass transit, the walkability to restaurants and retail, conference centers, fitness facilities and other important amenities. The office space itself has become a key recruiting and retention tool for employers seeking to hire and keep talented workers with the design, through efficiency and productivity, playing an important role in employee satisfaction.

CHAPTER 4

INDUSTRIAL

Imagine a one-story building that has 1 million square feet (nearly 23 acres) under its roof – a facility that's 2,000 feet long (more than six football fields) and 500 feet wide which can span the length of an entire city block. Industrial buildings can easily be that big – or even larger.

Walmart warehouse distribution building
1,114,000 square feet

There are two types of buildings under the industrial category umbrella: industrial and manufacturing. Industrial buildings are primarily for product distribution. Manufacturing buildings are used in the actual development and building of the products.

Industrial/Distribution Use

The design, functionality, and use of industrial buildings has changed dramatically over the years. Today's users are demanding bigger facilities with higher clear-height (the span between the building slab and the lowest joist in the ceiling) so they can pack more products into the space. At the same time, cities have gotten much more particular about how industrial buildings blend into their communities, so newer developments are cleaner and better landscaped. If master-planned properly, industrial developments can peacefully co-exist near residential neighborhoods and provide a terrific tax base for cities.

Warehouse built in 1968

Warehouse built in 2013

To understand industrial space, it helps to know a little bit about the supply chain, or how products are distributed. Manufacturers all over the world ship their products in TEUs, or Twenty Equivalent

Units. You've no doubt seen these containers on freighter (cargo) ships and railroad cars.

From seaports all over the world, these containers are delivered by ship to Tier I cities like Chicago, Los Angeles, Atlanta, Ft Lauderdale, etc. Then they are shipped by train or truck to intermodal yards – interior, land-based ports. (For trips of 500 miles or greater, it's cheaper to send by train due to the cost of fuel).

Products are then shipped to a warehouse for distribution, by either train or truck, before being delivered to stores or consumers. The demand for speed to the end user is why Amazon, Target, Walmart, and other large retailers are all building huge warehouses in highly populated areas.

Industrial space is typically broken down into three basic types:

Big-Box Bulk

These buildings range from about 500,000 to 1 million square feet or more and have an interior finish (office space) of about 5 percent and land coverage of as high as 50 percent but as low as 40 percent. (A 500,000-square-foot building could need 1 million square feet of total land for outside truck yards and parking). They typically have a clear-height of 32 feet up to 40 feet or more. These buildings are used by Fortune 500 companies and e-commerce companies that distribute and sell a significant amount of products to consumers. Due to the size of these buildings, they generally have to be in large industrial parks that require a lot of land, which are on the outskirts of the major city markets.

1,100,000 square foot warehouse

Warehouse interior

Light Industrial-Distribution

These buildings range in size from about 200,000 square feet to 500,000 square feet. They have an interior finish of 5 percent to 25 percent and land coverage of 35 percent to 40 percent, with a clear height of 24 to 32 feet. These buildings are considered the "last mile" of the supply chain. These buildings, due to their smaller size, can be in parks within cities that are closer in to the consumer completing the distribution to the end user. Amazon may have a 1 million square foot building on the outskirts of a city in a large industrial park but then have one or more smaller facilities for the quicker deliveries to the consumer to provide same or next day deliveries.

Greg Biggs

378,000 square foot warehouse

Flex Building/Small Warehouse/Call Centers

Facilities designed for these uses can be as small as about 20,000 square feet up to as large as 200,000 square feet. They can have as much as 50 to 100 percent interior finish with land coverage of 30 to 35 percent or more, depending on parking needs, and a clear height of 12 to 24 feet. These buildings house small, local and regional users for light manufacturing or office and distribution.

Two 60,000 square foot flex buildings

One of the advantages of developing and/or owning industrial product is that the refit of the interior of the building for a new tenant, should the existing tenant move out, is significantly less expensive than office building refit costs. Additionally, the cost of developing an industrial building is much less than the cost of developing office space.

Besides the quality of the building, a few other factors are important to consider when developing industrial space. Locations that provide access to major highways and rail spurs are critical. Solid soil, for the building slab integrity, is also important. (Bad dirt can ruin the usability of a building). Electric power can also be important to the success of a project, depending on user needs.

Manufacturing Use

A large amount of manufacturing that was originally done in the United States has since been relocated to Asia or countries like Mexico where the labor is significantly less expensive, which helps produce the products at a cheaper cost. Manufacturing also got a bad reputation due to some plants polluting and contaminating the environment around their facilities. Consequently, although there is still manufacturing that is done in the US, the environmental restrictions are significant and the locations where heavy manufacturing can take place is well outside most community boundaries.

Manufacturing buildings are built to the specifications of the manufacturer of the products. From the outside, these buildings typically look like distribution buildings. However, the interior is where the difference truly shows. These specifications include the overall size, height and slab (floor) load of the building, the amount of office required, the equipment needed for the manufacturing of the products and the storage space of the product until the distribution of the products takes place. These buildings rarely can be used as they were designed by a second tenant. They have to be redesigned and rebuilt to accommodate another user.

Manufacturing interiors

CHAPTER 5

DATA CENTERS

Data centers are one of the most expensive real estate products built and operated. The reason is simple: Data centers house the backbone of corporate and governmental technology infrastructure, where redundancy and connectivity are critical. Users can't have their mission critical facilities go down, and the level of criticality of the company's information determines the potential level of spend on the data center, as there are varying degrees of facility quality.

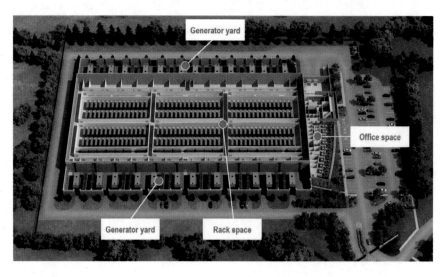

Skybox Data Center

There are, at a high level, two types of data centers: enterprise owned and third-party. Enterprise owned data centers are single-tenant centers occupied by major corporations like Bank of America, Microsoft, and Goldman Sachs.

Third-party data centers providers own or master-lease the data center facility and rent suites, small cages, cabinets or even servers out to end-users. They also manage and operate the supporting infrastructure. There are three different types of third-party providers: colocation (colo), hosting and managed services.

Colo providers will lease to multiple tenants who are responsible for their own information technology (IT) equipment (racks, servers and software) within the leased space. Digital Realty, QTS and CyrusOne are examples of colo providers.

Hosting providers build the environment and also take care of and manage the IT equipment. IBM and Rackspace are examples of hosting providers.

Managed services firms maintain and manage the IT equipment, but also manage the software and connectivity for the tenant, taking on all functions of the tenant's technology needs. Hewlett Packard, Dell and Perot Systems are all companies that provide managed services for data center users, along with IBM which does both.

The infrastructure of a data center has three critical components: power, cooling, and connectivity. The power required for data centers is substantial compared to a typical office or industrial building.

An average office building is designed for 8 to 12 watts of electricity per square foot for the tenants use, whereas a data center is designed for 150 - 250 watts per square foot.

Rack space

Cooling is also critical for data centers. With the amount of power consumed by these buildings and the residing IT equipment, they have to be continually cooled with massive air-conditioning systems in order to keep the IT equipment operating.

The connectivity, or fiber optic connections, allow the data centers and consumers of the data to communicate with one another. Ancillary systems like fire suppression, raised flooring and security are also important pieces of a data center facilities build-out.

Data center infrastructure and their redundancy are described in Tier levels. They range from Tier I through Tier IV. Tier I is the least redundant with Tier IV being the most redundant, virtually eliminating any chance of downtime for the center. Redundant power provides extra or spare power for a data center as back-up for power outages. The level or rating of Tier also determines cost to build and operate the facility which effectively determines the lease rates for an end-user.

Generator yard

The data center industry has been experiencing robust growth and will continue to boom, as business and personal use of data exponentially expands. A number of U.S. markets have emerged as data center hot spots, due to minimal risk for factors like dramatic weather (tornados, hurricanes or earthquakes), easy access to low cost power, major internet peering points and other factors. The current top five markets are northern Virginia and Washington, D.C.; Santa Clara/San Jose, and South Bay, California; northern New Jersey; Chicago; and Dallas-Fort Worth.

CHAPTER 6

RETAIL

Merriam-Webster's definition of retail is to sell something (a product) to customers for their own use. Think about how much retail real estate you are exposed to on a daily basis. You can't drive down the street without seeing a retail vendor who is trying to sell you something, gas stations, donut stores, cell phone companies, clothing companies, restaurants, fast food joint, banks.....you get the point.

Retail real estate is one of the more complex product types of commercial real estate because the number of categories and subcategories is significant and the ownership of these different categories and subcategories of retail have different investment strategies. For this chapter, we will discuss some of the major types of retail uses.

Malls

Shopping malls were established in Ancient Rome and originated in the forums where the markets were located. In ancient societies, shops were located along one thoroughfare or in one marketplace. If you fast-forward 2,000 years, the concept of a shopping mall is still alive and at work, but in a much bigger and more uniform way, in the modern shopping mall.

In America, an early indoor prototype was built in Minnesota in 1915. It was called the Lake View Store. It was a three-story building with stores on every level. The first self-contained, open-air mall, Highland Park Village, opened in Dallas in 1931.

With the rise of the automobile and suburban living, a new style of shopping center was created – built farther way from a city's downtown. Tax incentives encouraged investors to band together and build shopping malls. It was a win-win economically and functionally for people in the suburbs and corporate investors.

As shopping patterns have evolved, malls have suffered recently and are trying to reinvent themselves. Like other forms of real estate, they can be broken down into different classes. Class A malls are dominant properties in major metro areas. They're typically anchored by high-end stores such as Sak's Fifth Avenue and Neiman Marcus. Class B malls are non-dominant competitors in their trade areas.

Northpark Mall

Big Box

Big Box users are considered such because of the size of the building, typically 75,000 – 150,000 square feet. They can stand alone or be the primary tenant in a larger development. Stores such as Home Depot, Target, K-Mart and Walmart are examples of the big box tenant users.

Ikea Store

Retail Anchors

Retail anchors are typically 25,000 to 50,000 users like Dick's Sporting Goods, Best Buy and Havertys Furniture Store. They are typically the largest tenant in a retail center but not the only one.

Junior Anchors

Junior anchors make up the remaining tenant base in retail centers led by the retail anchors.

Dick's and Toys-R-Us retail anchors | Junior anchors in between

In-line or small shop retail

These are your smaller centers that house users like UPS, Metro PCS, nail salons and the like. Typically, these users are 1,000 – 3,000 square feet.

In-line retail

Entertainment

Newer venues like Main Event, high end bowling alleys and upscale movie theaters are all recent types of standalone entertainment venues that are becoming very prevalent across the country.

Main Event Entertainment center

Greg Biggs

Restaurants

As you can imagine, there are many different types of restaurants. Quick Service Restaurants (QSR's), are "order at the counter and take the food with you to go" or you can sit down to eat in the restaurant. McDonalds, Burger King and Taco Bell are examples of QSR's. Fast casual are restaurants where you order at the counter and your order is brought to you, somewhat better quality food or healthier food. Examples include diners like Genghis Grill, Panera Bread, Zoe's Kitchen and Chipotle. Casual dining is when you order at the table and your order is served to you, but it is not overly expensive. Chilies, Applebee's, Red Lobster, Olive Garden and On the Border are all examples of casual dining restaurants. Luxury restaurants serve high end food and beverages with high end service. The Capital Grill, Morton's The Steakhouse, and Ruth's Chris Steakhouse are all examples of luxury restaurants.

CHAPTER 7

HOSPITALITY

In commercial real estate, hospitality is primarily thought of as hotels. However, the hospitality industry includes convention centers, conference centers, residence clubs, spas, casinos and specialty settings like cruise ships.

For the purposes of this book we will focus on the hotel industry. Hotel real estate has two unique differences from the other products of commercial real estate.

1. The tenant base is primarily daily. Most other products, except medical, are focused on getting multi-year leases from their tenants.

2. While hotels have land and a building (traditional real estate), they have a huge operating component which is the central premise to the business of hospitality.

Hotels tend to have a dramatic social aspect to them. Guests stay largely from what someone else wants them to do. Ask yourself this, "Why do I stay in a hotel?" They are designed to attract people for weddings, vacations, honeymoons, family reunions, conventions and business meetings. They employ a significant amount of people in the restaurants, spas, bars, lunch and dinner business, valet service and day-to-day management of the hotel. They also have a dramatic effect on the neighborhood especially in a mixed-use project.

Hotels can be owned by Real Estate Investment Trusts (REITS), publicly traded companies, families or individuals, cities or municipalities, pension or equity firms or private partnerships. Although these may be the owners of the hotels, the success of a hotel is much more about the operating company that runs the day-to-day business than it is the real estate, although like all real estate projects, location is important.

Hotels are typically classified by brand, sometimes referred to as the flag, and recognized by quality. There are over 500 hotel brands worldwide. See the following graph:

Typical categorization of hotels

 **BUDGET** Economy	• Clean, simple accommodations • No food & beverage (F&B) or food service (FS) • Targets the budget-conscious leisure travelers and transient worker (truck drivers, as an example)	
LIMITED SERVICE Value	• Functional and nicely appointed accommodations • May offer buffet breakfast service, but not likely to have other F&B • Targets the budget-conscious business traveler	
MIDSCALE Quality	• Quality rooms • On-property F&B and some FS • Amenities such as fitness facilities and lobby retail shop • Targets all segments, particularly group travel	
UPSCALE Superior	• Attractive and highly functional guest rooms with business support amenities • Multiple F&B outlets and substantial FS • Targets business traveler and other convention groups	
LUXURY Exceptional	• High-end rooms and top-grade amenities • Restaurants and bars • Moderate to extensive FS • Targets executive-class business traveler and first-class leisure travelers • Minimal group business	

Budgets hotels are clean and simple, typically not having any type of food service. They target budget-conscious leisure travelers and transient workers.

Limited service hotels are functional and in some cases provide nicely appointed accommodations. Most of them offer a buffet breakfast service but don't have other food services.

Mid-scale hotels target all segments of customers but focus primarily on group travel. This level of hotel starts to have more amenities like fitness facilities and retail lobby shops in addition to nicer food and beverage service.

Upscale hotels have attractive and highly functional guestrooms with business support amenities. They will also have multiple food and beverage options with substantial food service. These hotels target the business traveler primarily but also cater to convention groups.

Luxury hotels have high-end rooms with top quality amenities. They typically have more than one restaurant and bar that often attract non-guests. They typically have extensive food service capabilities. Their target market are the executive-class business traveler and first class leisure travelers.

CHAPTER 8

HEALTHCARE

In years past, most medical healthcare was conducted within hospitals or within the campus that housed the hospital. This is still a very common practice across the U.S. However, with the changes in the national healthcare laws and continued improvements in the medical field, more and more specialty type uses have emerged.

These changes in the healthcare business have created numerous changes in the real estate that houses the businesses. Besides general (traditional) hospitals, there are acute care hospitals, ambulatory surgery centers (ASC's), out-patient clinics, mental health hospitals, sleep labs, physical therapy/rehab centers, skilled nursing facilities and medical office buildings (MOB's).

There are two types of buildings that house these different uses, stick-built (residential type construction) and commercial (tilt-wall or mid-rise construction). The stick-built type is usually smaller, single story buildings (5,000 square feet to 12,000 square feet) and are wood framed with brick exterior. This residential style of building is more likely to house a single tenant user giving the perception that the tenant owns the building, which can be equated to having a more successful practice. Often times, the doctors will own the building, as many of these medical offices are developed as office condo projects allowing physicians to purchase their suite or building. The purchase process and ownership structure is analogous to that of a residential condominium building.

The commercial type structures (12,000 square feet and up) are typically multiple stories and are more likely to accommodate multiple healthcare tenants of varying uses. These correlate more closely to the on campus MOB's in layout and construction but are usually smaller in scale. Typically these buildings follow a more traditional lease model. Leases will often range between seven to ten years for new medical leases in brand new buildings. The length of the term is often a product of the exorbitant cost of construction for medical office finish outs. Second generation medical offices will likely accommodate much shorter terms, often in the three to five year range.

With construction costs on a consistent upward trajectory, redevelopment and repurposing existing structures has become a popular way to save costs. Many older buildings trade at a reduced value and will usually be significantly cheaper than the cost of new construction. Even well known retailers like Blockbuster and Circuit City, that vacated locations across the country, became targets for medical office redevelopments.

In the past, healthcare tenants would be at the back of the hospital campus and not at the forefront because healthcare was not a drive up business but was driven by referrals. However, prominence has become much more important to physicians, and metrics like traffic counts, demographics and visibility are viewed in equal importance to the previous determining factors of referral patterns and hospital proximity. Prime locations have become paramount. Specialty healthcare businesses like dermatology, optometry, dental surgery centers and orthopedic surgery centers are now much more interested in being in prime locations like main intersection corners than ever before.

From left to right, surgery center, dialysis center, and a combination dermatology center, cosmetic laser surgery Center and dental building.

CHAPTER 9

MULTI-FAMILY

There are a number of multi-family property types that provide housing for all types of residents, from student housing on college campuses to high-rise living in urban centers to senior housing facilities. Lately, the demand for multi-family space across a variety of sectors has strengthened, as millennials put off home ownership and as baby boomers opt for the convenience of a rental lifestyle.

From an investment perspective, multi-family real estate is very popular with institutional buyers like pension funds and life insurance companies because the recurring cash flow is very predictable allowing the investors to hold the projects for a longer period of time. This creates a predictable return for the investors and a hedge against inflation.

Apartments

Apartment complexes are rental opportunities that provide single or multiple bedroom rental units. They cater to all types of residents, from blue-collar workers to the wealthy. The difference is driven by the construction type and amenities, and is reflected in the rent that is charged. Parking is also a driver for cost and function of the style of units. Apartments typically have annual leasing programs.

New ground-up development is the most popular type of multi-family value creation. Redevelopment, or repositioning, is booming in many downtown areas, as renters are seeking urban lifestyles. For redevelopment or repositioning investors, the goal is to pay a lot less than replacement cost for a complex, then invest a certain amount of capital per unit to refurbish the space. Functional obsolescence can be a challenge with many older apartment complexes. Ceiling heights, utility and washer and dryer connections or locations of the apartments and safety are all things to consider when redeveloping or repositioning projects.

RE150 Complex | 282 Units

Condominiums

Condominiums are units that are bought and sold individually. They can be high-rise units or low-rise units. Condominiums will have a homeowner's association (HOA) to facilitate the management and decisions of the common areas for the building and its individual owners. Condos are higher risk from a development standpoint because they can be difficult to finance. They sell better where single family-housing is less affordable.

Museum Tower 42 stories

Student Housing

Student housing properties, as you might guess, are traditionally close to universities, but located off campus and rent by the bedroom with a common area in each unit, similar to what you'd find in a hotel. The schools themselves provide dormitory units and are the biggest competition for this type of housing development. Some universities, are now starting to partner with third-party developers to do on-campus residential projects. Student housing leasing revolves around the school year as most students go home during the summer. If your project is not leased up when school starts, your chances of additional leasing are significantly low.

University of Texas at Dallas

Senior Housing

Senior housing is a highly specialized form of multi-family real estate, with projects that provide varying levels of care. Some properties are strictly residential and don't include any additional services. Others provide lifestyle amenities such as food services. There are also assisted care properties and others that provide Alzheimer's care and age-restricted care. Developers of these facilities have the extra responsibility of staffing not only the leasing and property management personnel, but also healthcare providers for the residents.

Highland Springs Senior Housing in Dallas, TX

CHAPTER 10

MIXED-USE

A mixed-use project is a master development with a mixture of allowable uses. Modern day mixed-use developments were inspired from the idea of "live, work and play" communities. Today's mixed-use developments might include a mixture of office, retail, multi-family, entertainment (i.e., a cinema or bowling alley), and hotel. Some of these developments house upwards of 10,000 employees and residents.

Mixed-use developments are much more complicated than a single use development. A mixed-use project can be much more challenging to design, finance, and build out due to the complexities of integrating each individual use within the project. Multiple architects, financial institutions, and general contractors must be coordinated to achieve the overall goal of success.

Legacy North

Another example of mixed-use development is in the medical field for integrated health campuses where there is a hospital, retail, and a hospitality component.

Presbyterian Hospital Plano

The key to mixed-use developments is how it is all integrated for walkability. Due to the number of people who can be housed in these developments, parking is also always a concern which is why developers often look to develop mixed-use projects in close proximity to mass transit stations. However, if mass transit is not available, special attention must be paid toward the parking and how it can accommodate the users of every component of the mixed-use development.

Galleria Dallas

CHAPTER 11

ARCHITECTURE

Webster's definition of architecture is "The art or science of designing and creating buildings." However, there is so much more to architecture than this. It's often said you can create your own career after obtaining a design degree. At times, architects act as inventors, educators, sales people, developers, strategists, advisers and coaches; sometimes they are all of these in one day!

Architects transform the world around us today using modern technology for planning, designing and overseeing the ultimate construction of their projects.

Each real estate project typically starts with a client need. Clients include corporations or users of every type of commercial space, along with developers, investors and owners. A client can be anyone that has a dream to create a space and the financial capability to bring the project to reality. The architect listens to the client and learns what type of space the client seeks to build.

Architecture is an innovative, multifaceted industry and an extremely rewarding profession in which you can clearly see the results of your work. Not many professions allow you to point to a project that you had a hand in that has an impact on the way people live, work and play. It's a truly priceless feeling to know you had a hand in creating something for others to enjoy.

It's also a dynamic industry. The way people work is always evolving, and there is never a "final" or "right" answer. Architects are always experimenting with their designs, as architecture is constantly changing, which means architects are always learning.

A career in architecture incorporates artistic interpretation and architectural preciseness while balancing business and client relationships. Businesses evolve, cultures adapt to new influences and technology evolves faster than we can keep up. This means that clients will always have new and unique needs. One of the most rewarding parts of the job is getting to know the clients on a deep level; their culture, their goals, the DNA of their organization. Knowing your clients and their business inside and out helps you provide more valuable services to them and also helps you to become a well-rounded and well-versed professional.

Architecture has a professional apprenticeship of about two to three years before a student can have enough hours of training and numerous rigorous exams to obtain his or her license to practice architecture. The apprenticeship is set up for a good reason, as there are things about how a building comes together that can only be learned in the real world. In school you will learn about the theories of design, professional practice and some engineering coordination, but as soon as you start working for an architecture firm, you will start putting those theories and teachings into practice. The learning curve is getting shorter than it has in years past, but it still takes time for a person coming out of school to understand everything that is needed to build a building. That is why they call it the "practice" of architecture; you're always learning.

Students who study architecture must be committed to the rigorous degree programs, which require a great deal of studio time. Courses have evolved to better gear students to be prepared when entering the workforce. We are in a digital age in which technology will only continue to improve, so computer and graphics expertise is important.

Architecture firms look for creative, thoughtful, talented individuals, who are enthusiastic and energetic, possess drive, ambition, and passion…people who love to learn and are curious. They also want a person with a keen ability to focus with a clear understanding of who they are and what they want, with a well-rounded balance of technical, writing, and interpersonal skills. It's not enough to be "book smart" in the industry. Being comfortable when interacting with people and their different personalities is crucial for success. You will also need to be a good listener, be able to reserve judgment and put yourself in the shoes of many other people to truly understand what's important. To advance within a firm, most architecture firms require the employee to have their license.

A collaborative spirit is imperative to work in a team environment. A young person should be able to articulately explain and present his or her body of work. Architecture firms also look for students who are well rounded, confident and show interest and involvement in extracurricular activities. Public speaking classes and business classes are suggested along with the requirements of a design degree. Possessing business acumen will advance a career. Last, but not least: DISCIPLINE!

The American Institute of Architecture (AIA) is a terrific resource if you are interested in the Architecture field. www.aia.org

CHAPTER 12

DEVELOPMENT

There are developers of every product type of real estate. However, there are different types of developers. They include; 1. Speculative developers, ones that will build a product without a tenant in hopes that a future tenant will want to lease what the developer builds, 2. Single tenant developers, ones that build a project having an agreement with a user to either lease or buy the building and 3. Investment developers that build a building for their own, or an investor clients, long term hold account.

Developers have three types of customers:

1. Users that lease their product,

2. Users that buy the product,

3. Investors that want a project built to lease to users for their investment account.

As a developer, you have to stay focused on the customers' needs and look for trends that the customers want to buy. As in most business, customer service is critical to the development business.

The steps to developing a successful project are numerous. Developers have to make 50,000 decisions. Most have to be made on the spot which is why the learning curve in the development business is relatively steep. A long and distinguished resume is usually instrumental in establishing the confidence of the investors, end users and financing sources.

Development is a team sport. Some developers have teams of employees, including marketing personnel, construction management personnel, architects, leasing people, etc. Some developers choose to keep their staff small. The difference in size is typically due to their particular business model and focus of their business.

There can be crushing blows along the way. A successful developer has to be able to get up every day and solve problems that always arise on projects. When dealing with city governments including mayors, city councils, zoning departments, even fire marshals, you must have patience and an understanding of what is important to each person or group you will be dealing with. You must always deliver on what you promise! Governmental employees, elected officials, tenants and financial institutions tend to have long memories.

Correctly underwriting the risk is the key to a successful development. You must be able to have the ability to raise investment money, finance and build a project. To do that effectively, you will need training by spending time in the field on projects that you find interesting. If you can work for a company that can teach you about construction, budgets, debt, equity, leverage, property management and the importance of selecting the right partners, it will increase your chances of success dramatically. If you want to start your own firm one day, your development education could take years and years but like most disciplines, being able to survive in the good and especially the bad times is how you build a career which means you may want to work for someone else for a down cycle or two to learn what a down cycle truly means.

While most developers typically make the "Big Pop" when they sell their project, one successful multi-family developer never goes into a project to sell it. He develops his projects to lease them up and meet his partners expected annual return parameters after he puts permanent debt on the project. He only sells projects when a buyer offers what he can't turn down, usually in an up-cycle of the market.

The credit of the tenant/tenants is very important to developers for a number of reasons. Primarily they want to make sure the tenants will be around to pay the rent over the term of the lease or write the final check if the client is buying the building. It is also important for financing the project. Additionally, should the developer want to sell the building, the tenant's credit will be an important part of the formula for the final value of the project.

From the types of projects they build to the ownership structures they have to the teams they hire developers are very different from one another. Should you choose to enter this field, you should learn as much as you can about their history and competitive advantage before engaging in a job search.

A well-rounded education of finance, people skills, patience, tenacity, legal and real estate vision are all traits that are needed for the development side of the business. Like other service lines, most developers will educate you on their way of doing the business but if you can stand out in any of the above traits you will make a positive impression in your interviews.

The Commercial Real Estate Development Association (NAIOP) www.naiop.org is a great resource for the development business.

CHAPTER 13

CONSTRUCTION

Construction is one of those services that has many disciplines under its umbrella. The bottom line for a construction company is to build the vision of the owner/tenant that the architects and engineers design and bring it to life on time and on budget without sacrificing quality.

The larger construction companies (General Contractors, GC's) may have thousands of employees covering many different jobs on a national scale. These GC's focus on core and shell (the base building) and interiors construction (the tenant improvements). Smaller firms typically focus on one of those specialties.

Construction has a finite life cycle which means that companies have to continually market for new business. Being finite, the construction business continually needs to be fed with new business. Construction companies often are challenged to balance keeping their teams constantly busy while being careful not to over commit on their ability to complete new business.

GC's usually have to bid for a job. Most of the time, it is a competitive bid against other GC's although there are times when a client will just award a construction contract to a trusted GC. This can happen when time is of the essence more than normal or the client understands the costs so well that they just negotiate with the GC without the competitive bid process and in this case the GC has become trusted by the owner.

GC's are responsible for the delivery of the contracted project. They work with subcontractors (subs) like electrical, plumbing, drywall, lighting, painting, HVAC (Heating, ventilation and air conditioning), flooring, concrete, glass and landscaping. The GC will be provided the plans, specifications, and the expected timing of the project that the architect and engineer have created to multiple subs and have them bid their portion of the job with the low bidder usually being awarded the work. Once the GC has all of the bids in, the GC will "level" the subcontractors' bids and submit their lowest bid to the owner/client. It's not uncommon for subcontractors to bid with multiple GC's. Owners and clients typically get bids from multiple GC's then make the final selection of the GC to be on their team.

Employees at a GC's company include account executives, project managers, project engineers, estimators, superintendents and safety managers. These are the people who are involved with the day to day construction of the project. There are also management, business development, accounting and operation personnel to run the day to day business of the company.

With so many different positions within a construction company, it is difficult to provide a typical skill set for the construction field. However, people with degrees in Construction Management, Architecture, Engineering or just an aptitude for understanding construction can get a GC's attention. GC's will tell you that they are always on the lookout for good talent.

National commercial construction companies include Structuretone, Balfour Beatty, Turner, Skanska, Holder, McCarthy, DPR, Jacobs, Whiting Turner and Gilbane. All of the big national firms will have an HR department that will know what jobs they are looking to fill.

Other opportunities within the construction field include project management. Most commercial real estate companies have project management in house to act as the tenant's representative to oversee construction projects and to manage work done between the architect and the general contractor to ensure the budget and timeline are maintained. Job opportunities at these companies will be looking for the same background as GC's.

The Associated Contractors of America (AGC) is a great resource for the construction business.

CHAPTER 14

OWNERSHIP - INVESTMENT

The bottom line in ownership of real estates, as any investment, is to make a profit. To buy low and sell high, or build for a tenant, or tenants, at a total construction cost number and then sell it higher for a return that meets or exceeds investor expectations. As simple as it sounds, a lot of people have lost a lot of money in bad real estate investments. Of course, a lot of people have made a lot of money as well.

Real estate has become a much more popular investment than ever before. Properties are tangible assets. Commercial real estate assets typically offer higher yields, serve as a hedge against inflation, and diversify investment exposure away from traditional asset classes. Investors looking to real estate for diversification typically focus on "risk adjusted returns", which generally refer to getting more bang (yield) for risk (volatility). Diversification is a primary driver for investors looking to preserve wealth, less of a driver for investors looking to create wealth.

The capitalization rate (cap rate) is the most commonly used valuation metric for real estate. It is calculated as the ratio between the net operating income produced by an asset and the original capital cost (the price paid to buy the asset) or alternatively its current market value. The lower the cap rate the more expensive the property. The formula is the annual net operating income or the net rentals realized by the owner divided by the current market value or sales price = cap rate.

Example: An apartment building sells for $300,000.

The rental income after expenses (net) are $24,000.
$24,000 / $300,000 = .08 creating the 8% Cap Rate

In addition to cap rate, other metrics for real estate purchases are: price per square foot for office, industrial and retail assets and price per unit for multi-family assets.

There are five types of owners for commercial real estate:

1. Institutional Owners: These are pension funds like Vanguard, Teachers Insurance and Annuity Association College Retirement Equities Fund (TIAA-CREF), California State Teachers Retirement System (CalSTRS), and Tennessee Consolidated Retirement System. Insurance companies like MetLife, Prudential, State Farm, Principal Financial Group and USAA are big owners of commercial real estate. Institutional owners try to have a certain percentage of their total assets invested in real estate, typically 6 to 10 percent.

2. Private Equity Funds: The Largest private equity fund is Blackstone Group which is a $344 billion dollar investment firm. Other large funds include Kohlberg Kravis Roberts (KKR) and JP Morgan. Smaller private equity funds will invest upwards of $50 million in assets. Funds will have different investment strategies within their portfolios as it relates to the real estate portion of their fund. As an example, some funds will invest in core assists, value-add / opportunistic, or debt-related. Core assets are typically well occupied with high-quality tenants that have staggered lease expirations. They are well maintained and are located in high-quality, high-barrier-to-entry markets such as New York, Washington D.C., Boston, San Francisco, Los Angeles, and other large metropolitan areas where quality space is scarce and new development is difficult. The main property types include office, retail, multi-family and industrial. Value-add / opportunistic funds seek out under-performing (in their opinion) assets and attempt to solve the problems with the asset to enhance the value. The property challenges can be physical, functional, operational and /or financial which typically create vacancies in the property. They hope to buy the property at substantial discount and by correctly identifying and addressing the issues for the property, the fund hopes to realize larger returns once the property is stabilized. Debt-related funds have increased in popularity due to the lack of availability of bank financing. Many fund managers are stepping in

to provide the funding gap for real estate. These funds believe that they can generate returns with a lower level of risk than equity investments.

3. Corporations: Numerous corporations choose to own their real estate instead of leasing it. Walmart is one of the largest owners of real estate in the world.

4. High Net Worth: High net worth individuals and families often invest in real estate. Families like Trump, Perot, Crow, Hines, LeFrak, Speer and Ross have significant real estate holdings in different types of products.

5. REITS. REITS are real estate investment trusts that are publicly held and are invested in through the purchase of stock. These are companies that are modeled after mutual funds providing investors with regular income streams, diversification and long-term capital appreciation. REITs typically pay out all of their taxable income as dividends to shareholders who then are responsible for the taxes on those dividends. While most REITs are traded on the major stock exchanges, there are also public non-listed and private REITs. There are two main types of REITs: Equity REITs that generate income from the rent on and sales of the properties they own and Mortgage REITs that invest in mortgages tied to the real estate.

6. Governments: The US government is a large owner of real estate. The governmental organization that facilitates

the government's real estate is the General Services Administration (GSA, www.gsa.gov).

Careers in ownership may include development, construction, leasing, property management and research analytics.

CHAPTER 15

CAPITAL MARKET SALES

The capital markets side of the business includes real estate sales and financing (debt and equity placements). Selling and/or providing debt and/or equity on a commercial property is what gives real estate professionals that specialize in capital markets the opportunity to provide value.

A broker who specializes in selling an asset typically has to compete for the opportunity to sell the property. The property owner will usually invite capital market teams to make presentations so that the owner can learn of the team's experience, their expectations of pricing, the potential buyer pool and the chemistry of their team. Once the owner has selected and hired the preferred broker or team, the broker will create a marketing package. These packages can be very elaborate depending on the significance and price of the property. Sometimes, properties are sold in packages (multiple properties) of similar type products. Occasionally they are in multiple cities. For big institutional investors, it's a great way to place large amounts of funds into real estate at one time. With that in mind, you can see how the marketing packages can be significant. The packages will include at a minimum a description of the property, an aerial view, multiple pictures, the tenant rent role, future assumptions and market overview. Once the packages have been sent to the prospective buyer pool, the brokerage team will work with the potential buyers to help them understand the opportunity in buying the property or properties. After the potential buyers complete their due diligence, offers will be submitted. Then, the broker will analyze the initial offers and work with the top bidders to improve their offers for a best and final bid submission. Once the seller and buyer have agreed to all of the terms of the sale and both have signed the contract, the property is formally "under contract." If all goes well, the closing date is set and the buyer funds the sale.

Very few commercial real estate projects are purchased with 100% cash. The majority have debt against the property from a lending source who in return requires the owner to have a certain amount of equity (the borrower's money or their partnerships money) invested in the project. Ownership entities of commercial real estate can be set up in many different partnership structures and financial arrangements. This is how brokers who specialize in financing can add value.

The financing side of the brokerage business is very similar to investment sales. The primary difference is that in most scenarios the financing broker represents the "buyer" versus the investment sales broker is representing the "seller." The financing side of the brokerage business works closely with the investment sales brokerage process. The financing broker structures the debt and equity capital needed for an investor to acquire the property the Investment sales broker is selling.

The pitch process for a financing broker is very similar to the pitch process for investment sales brokers. They have to make presentations detailing experience, the status of the capital markets (the lending market, interest rates, etc.), and discuss the market of potential lenders for the potential acquisition. Once a financing broker has procured an assignment, he creates a marketing package very similar to that of an investment sales broker, but with a greater emphasis on the financial status of the property. As opposed to sending the marketing package to potential buyers, the financing broker will send the package to potential lenders or capital sources (life insurance companies, CMBS, banks, credit companies, pension funds, private equity or high net worth families). The financing broker adds value by getting the lenders or capital sources interested in the deal/transaction and pushing them to offer the most competitive financing (the "loan") on the subject property for the borrower (the "buyer or investor"). This process usually consists of the financing broker negotiating financing terms (interest rates, fees, etc.) with each of the interested lenders. Once the broker has finalized terms, the buyer/borrower will select a lender. The lender will then analyze the credit of the borrower and the tenant base and if there is one, assuming all goes well, the lender will fund their portion of the loan allowing the borrower to close on the property on the closing date agreed to with the seller.

Having a good understanding of financial modeling will help when being considered for a position within a capital markets group. A business degree in finance with a focus in real estate would be ideal but not a must. If you are a hard-working self-starter with an under-standing of finance and join a firm that has a good training program, the firm will teach you in the first 24 months what you will need to know for a long career in this field. A distinguishing feature as to your progress in interacting with clients will be your people skills. Some in the field remain an analyst for their entire career and are totally fine with that profession. Others are able to progress through the years to the "first chair" of selling, interacting with the clients, negotiating with buyers and ultimately closing the deals.

CHAPTER 16

LEASING

There are two types of commercial project leasing roles: in-house for an owner of property and for a company that provides third party leasing services to owners of property. Owners typically utilize third party leasing companies because they don't carry the staff, in-house to lease their projects for any number of reasons. Third party leasing agents usually have to compete for their leasing assignments against other third party firms. For a third party firm, successfully selling their leasing services is just the first step in securing revenue from the business.

As a leasing agent, your job is to sell your clients product, a tangible asset, to a user (lessor/tenant) of real estate. Your primary responsibility is to convince the users that your project is the best possible alternative for them to house their business. To do that, you will need to intimately know the supply and demand of your market as well as understand the goals and objectives your client (the owner) is trying to achieve.

Leasing space requires thoughtfulness and hard work. It is imperative to understand the profile of the owner/client. The investor profile can range from an institutional owner to a public REIT to a local entrepreneur. Each will underwrite and value rental rates, lease term (length of lease), tenant credit and occupancy type differently. For example, a public REIT places significant value on the occupancy rate across their portfolio. All owners crave above-market rental rates, tenants with great credit, high occupancy and a long lease term, as those are the drivers that create the highest value for a real estate asset. It is important to understand your client's motivations in order to recommend a strategy and execution plan that provides a winning solution that aligns with your client's goals and objectives.

There are three key action items you can do in your preparation for your marketing effort and execution to be a successful leasing agent.

Preparation/homework will be critical to your success. Understanding the fundamental of the supply and demand of the market in general and of the immediate market of the client's property will be crucial. The supply side is all of the competitive blocks of space, both direct and sublease (space that is leased but the tenant is trying to dispose of because they no longer need it) blocks, and all competitive buildings to better understand their amenities, lobbies, parking garages, view corridors, ingress/egress, security and the design of the multi-tenant corridors. The competitions ownership, rental rates and vacancy history will also be important. The demand side will include all of the tenants currently in your immediate market and those looking for space. Learning what industry groups gravitate to your projects market and why will help as well. Second level preparation can include knowing the history of the properties ownership, the current debt structure and the existing tenant base. Also know the base lease form. Read it word-for-word and understand key clauses and provisions. A visit with the property manager and building engineer to gain knowledge of your building operating systems will help you know how the building management team operates, runs and maintains the asset.

Marketing of the asset will be of significant interest to the owner they will understand how you will position the asset in the market place. Promoting the strengths of your client will help in effort marketing. Steps like the leases being signed locally can save time. Also, the client being financially strong will provide confidence from the tenant so will know that the landlord will not have a problem funding tenant improvement allowances and other financial landlord obligations. Marketing Collateral to uniquely brand your asset will help it stand out to potential tenants. Knowing each of the vacant spaces in your project and how they are finished out will help you know in advance what will work for future tenants.

Having relationships with the tenant representatives in the market place will go a long way in helping drive tenants to your project.

Execution of your marketing efforts will drive success for leasing. Do everything you can to be responsive in timely returning calls and providing promised work as soon as possible. Be sure to know your path of a property tour before the tour takes place. Remember the names of all participants of the tour. If you can get a list of those attending and their titles within the company, that is even better. Ask the right questions and then LISTEN to learn as much as you can about what's important to the prospective tenant. Follow-up with the tenant's broker, or if they don't have one, the tenant is critical as it allows you to learn how the tour went and what you can do to further the tenant interest in your project.

In-house leasing personnel are often compensated with a base salary and a bonus or small commission structure. Third party leasing agents are typically paid a smaller salary with a larger commission structure.

Leasing agents have to do a lot of reporting and responding to request for proposals (RFP's). Having good-to-great sales capabilities and a proficiency in financial modeling in programs like Procalc and Excel will be helpful. Having your real estate license is a must for third party firms, however, in-house leasing agents don't necessarily have to have their license but you will want to check that point because the real estate laws differ from state to state.

CHAPTER 17

TENANT REPRESENTATION

Office buildings, industrial buildings, retail buildings and medical buildings all have tenants that occupy and lease space within those properties. Tenant representation specialists (tenant reps) work specifically with tenants, as their advocate, to assist them in determining where to locate their business and to help them in negotiating the terms and conditions of a lease or purchase of a property. Additionally, tenant reps serve as advisers to corporate users of real estate about their portfolios and various holdings.

Years ago, tenants were at a significant disadvantage because they were on their own when it came to negotiating their leases. They would deal with their lease every three, five or ten years or whenever their lease expired. It was more of a nuisance in doing business which gave landlords an advantage. Tenants needed someone that worked on their behalf that could help them through the real estate process, who created a competitive advantage for their tenancy, who worked in the market every day and who knew the current pricing for their particular property type.

In being a tenant representative, you are selling your service and expertise in your market knowledge, financial analysis, lease/contract document knowledge, negotiating skills and sales and presentation skills. It is a high risk, high reward business that can have some rough patches, but can be very lucrative over the long haul. Because of the potential for big commissions, there are usually a large number of practitioners in the larger markets but not a large number of players are at the top of the field. However, you can still make a very good living if you learn the skills to the business.

Besides being a lucrative discipline, tenant representatives get to work with many types of businesses and learn what makes them successful. It is also a very relational business in that you typically develop personal relationships with your clients as well as relationships with leasing agents, landlord representatives, developers, architects and attorneys, all of whom can also become clients.

The tenant rep business can be challenging for a number of reasons. In most real estate companies, tenant reps get compensated on a commission only basis. However, most firms understand that people with no experience will have to develop business that takes time and may provide a compensation structure to allow for a start-up period of time. But, recognize that start-up compensation will only last for a certain time.

Tenant representation requires patience and time management. It can take upwards of five years to establish the necessary skill set to compete in this overly competitive field. It will also help to be resilient! You get told "no" often as a tenant representative. The key to measuring success in the early stages in your career as a tenant rep is to experience consistent gains in your knowledge and skills as well as our economic production. You may not vault to the top of the profession early, but if you show consistent gains, then others in the industry will likely take notice, creating additional opportunities in the future.

In starting out in tenant representation, try to find a firm to work with that has a training program that gives you a well-rounded education about the real estate business. There are firms that specialize in tenant representation only and are considered boutique firms. While some find merit in this unique model, it is not a must to work for a tenant rep only firm as most of the major companies in the US have numerous disciplines which include tenant representation.

Finding a good mentor or an established team that needs someone for a particular job would also help you learn the business. As you start to understand the nuances of the daily tenant rep work load, find a way to make yourself invaluable to the senior people, learn what could be your niche. It shows initiative and a willingness to work hard.

Besides patience, typical characteristics needed for a successful tenant rep include:

- Good people skills

- Intelligence for financial modeling

- Capable of understanding legal language for contract / lease clauses

- Competitive fire

Tenant representation is very much a self-starter business. In preparation to finding that first job, you can take Certified Commercial Investment Member (CCIM) www.ccim.com classes to learn basic terminology and primary financial concepts that will be applicable in the business. A CCIM designation is a well-respected and recognized designation. Local commercial real estate associations may have commercial classes that may apply to the tenant rep business as well.

You will also need to be a licensed real estate broker so if you can find a sponsoring broker; you should proactively get your real estate license. If you don't have access to a sponsoring broker, you should take all of the courses you will need to obtain your license prior to or while interviewing.

CHAPTER 18

PROPERTY MANAGEMENT

Imagine a 70-story office tower in your downtown market. Did you know that as many as 6,000 people may work in a building of that size? Buildings don't just run themselves. They are like a smaller version of a city. Most of the services that it takes to run a city are included in the property management of a building. In fact, in a 70 story office tower, it may take a staff of as many as 30 people to run the building. Obviously smaller buildings require less staff but smaller buildings are no less important to their owners and the tenants who occupy them. A property manager has to be able to communicate on many different levels, from the owner of the building to the president of a company that is in the building to governmental inspectors to contractors to all of the third party vendors who service the building. A senior property manager also has to be a recruiter and a team builder. Having a cohesive team is very important to the successful day to day business of running a building.

The typical team under a senior property manager would include:

- A property administrator who is responsible for accounts receivable and payable

- A lease administrator who keeps track of all of the leases in the building and their different terms and conditions

- A chief engineer who is responsible for the systems in the building like the heating and air condition system, the elevators, the sprinkler system, etc.

- An accountant who is responsible for the financial reporting and calculations of the rents and depreciation schedules

- A variety of contractors. Contractors could include janitorial, security, window washing, pest control, landscaping, fire and life safety, parking management, telecommunications providers and other various service providers.

As you can see, a senior property manager has to have a level of expertise in many different areas as well as the ability to communicate expertly with each of the people who are involved with effectively running the building. The day to day activity of a property manager can vary greatly, from working with the owner to discussing budgets and the efficient management of the building to touring prospective tenants to negotiating a contract with a general contractor for the construction of space in the building – just to name a few of the possible daily activities.

Interestingly, most property managers don't start out on a carrier path for property management as their original goal. They typically come from other backgrounds where their skills are well suited for property management. For example, engineering, military back ground and technical training accounting/finance are all well qualified backgrounds for property management.

The most important thing to know about the property management field is that a property manager's job is never done. If you are one of those people that need task closure in your job, you may find this a frustrating field. There is always another report to write, one more inspection to make or one more meeting to schedule and attend. However, property managers can be compensated well. Most are compensated on a salary plus bonus program. Bonuses are generally established by performance measures where they can be bonused as much as 20% of the salary.

If the property management field is of interest to you, the best organization to investigate is the Building Owners and Managers Association, (BOMA) an international organization. At www. boma.org, you can learn about education opportunities and other issues that are important to the members of this important field. There are also designations you can investigate, the Real Property Administrator (RPA) and the Certified Property Manager (CPM).

CHAPTER 19

APPRAISAL

The appraisal business has long been a staple of the sales and lending side of the commercial real estate business. What you may not know is that appraisals are also used in litigation support, market rent studies by landlords and tenants, and governmental authorities for right of way work for utilities, roads and condemnations. They're also used for real estate investment trusts (REIT's), pension fund evaluations, both private investors and financial institutions, and feasibility studies for developers. In short, appraisers touch a lot of different real estate groups.

Appraisals, by definition, provide an expert opinion on the value of real properties. They are used to confirm or dis-affirm the values and conditions of the real estate asset or assets.

Appraisals are prepared in one of two separate formats – Appraisal Reports and Restricted Appraisal Reports – differing only in the amount of information communicated to the client; the supporting work file retained by the appraiser is the same for either.

Appraisals use three "approaches to value." The first is the "cost approach," which means the value of the land plus direct and indirect development costs for any improvements. This approach is primarily used for new development.

The "income approach" capitalizes income into value. The direct capitalization method relies on a formula loosely known as "IRV" – income divided by a market-supported cap rate equals the value. The yield capitalization method derives value by projecting cash flows into the future and then discounting them to present value.

The third method is the "sales approach," which typically uses four to eight sales comparables within the subject property's competitive market. From the appraiser's perspective, the report itself is generally broken into two halves. The "top half" includes, at a minimum, specifications like the legal description, property details, photos, site plans, relevant market data, property history and the recommended highest and best use. The "bottom half" of the report includes some combination of the three valuation approaches mentioned above to detail the estimated value of the property.

Being an appraiser is a very detail-oriented job. Necessary skills include proficiency in Word and Excel, writing composition and at least a general understanding of finance. An appraiser may work on one to ten appraisals a month, depending on complexity. The process usually begins when the entity requiring the appraisal requests a bid from the appraisal company. Bids are submitted based on price and the amount of time the appraiser requires to complete the assignment; the longer the amount of time given to perform the appraisal will typically yield better the pricing for the client, and vice versa. The winning bid is not always the lowest bid; in appraisal, as with any industry, you get what you pay for.

To legally work on appraisals, you must acquire an appraiser trainee license, which requires 75 hours of qualifying appraisal education and sponsorship by a Certified General Appraiser. If you want to practice appraisal on your own, you must obtain the Certified General Appraiser license, which requires no less than 3,000 experience hours, 300 education hours, a bachelor's degree and a passing grade on the eight-hour state license exam.

Beyond the state certification is the ultimate appraisal designation, the Designated Member of the Appraisal Institute (MAI). The MAI is one of the most respected designations in the real estate business. To obtain it, you must have an undergraduate degree from a four-year accredited university. There are more than 400 hours of classroom instruction that include 13 examinations (inclusive of all state general course-work, and an additional 140 hours of advanced course-work) followed by the general comprehensive exam, which is a month-long, four-part exam covering the most advanced concepts of valuation. Additionally, applicants must pass the "General Demonstration of Knowledge" requirement, and receive credit for 4,500 hours of specialized work over at least a three-year period. A detailed description of all MAI requirements is on the Appraisal Institute website, www.appraisalinstitute.org. As you can see, the MAI designation is very comprehensive, which is why it is so respected in the real estate field.

Due to recent changes in corporate accounting rules, public companies that have real property on their balance sheets have accounted for an increasing share of appraisal demand. These changes have since created numerous jobs at appraisal companies nationwide. The big four accounting firms will be staffing up to accommodate their client's needs as well.

Appraisal is regarded by many as the best foundational learning ground for commercial real estate, as professionals deal with sale contracts, leases, rent rolls, financial statements, construction budgets, buyers, sellers, tenants, brokers, developers, bankers, and more. Once you understand how property value is established, there are many different career paths that could open up to you, should you want to make a change.

CHAPTER 20

RESEARCH AND ANALYTICS

All major real estate companies utilize research and analytics to some degree. They either have research and analytics personnel in house or they use third party firms.

Research experts deliver information and insights on markets and economic activity, conditions, trends, forecasts and reports on where the market is now and where it is going. Real estate companies will have different requirements for research depending on the company's business. For example, a brokerage house will use research to help them differentiate themselves from their competitors to help them win business. An ownership firm will have their research group to help them determine whether an acquisition or development is in the right market or help underwrite the due diligence of a project. A developer will use research to determine the ultimate value of a project or help determine the next development site. An institutional owner will utilize their research team to publish letters about trends and opportunities in specific areas e.g. the benefits of commercial mortgages in a portfolio. They may also deliver weekly updates to management and provide strategic recommendations through annual presentation.

Research employees are expected to have the following skills:

- Superior creative writing and oral communication skills

- High-level analytical and problem-solving skills and strategic-thinking capacity

- Intellectual curiosity

- Passion and interest in real estate, the economy and markets overall

- Proficiency in Excel, Microsoft Power Point, Microsoft Word, CoStar and mapping technologies, such as ArcGIS

- Knowledge of macro- and micro-economic trends and their theoretical applications

Analytics is typically tied more to financial modeling and reporting. Similar to research, companies will have different uses for analytics depending on their revenue model. A brokerage house will use analytics in tenant representation, leasing and capital markets. Ownership firms and investment firms will use analytics to determine if a certain purchase makes financial sense or whether a certain lease obtains the Internal Rate of Return (IRR) they are trying to achieve in the project. A developer will use analytics to pro forma a future development to make sure that the project will make financial sense for investors, lenders and the tenant market.

Analytical employees are expected to be proficient in primarily Excel and Argus.

Starting your career in research and/or analytics could lead you to many different paths in the real estate industry. With such a high degree of exposure to many aspects of the commercial real estate industry, within two to three years, should you want to change your career path, you should be able to move to almost any service line with a background in research and analytics.

CHAPTER 21

LAUNCHING YOUR CAREER

Once you've decided that commercial real estate is for you, you can begin preparing for the launch of your career. This work will help you prepare for interviewing.

A good place to start is to get familiar with the companies in the discipline, cities and markets that interest you. There are a number of ways to go about this. Local chambers of commerce typically track this information. Local media outlets (business journals, magazines and newspapers) will report on commercial real estate news and may even produce research lists that rank the largest firms. Additionally, the local association of commercial realtors can be a great resource as well. If you have industry connections, leverage those as well.

Once you've pulled together a target list of companies that you would like to interview with, find out who the local manager or owner is and begin your research on them and their firm. This will be a real help in determining if there's a good fit. It's also helpful to know whether the company is a local (boutique), regional, national or global firm. The more research you do, the better prepared you'll be which will be greatly appreciated by the firm representatives that you meet. Your level of your research will demonstrate your interest in working with them.

Real Estate License

If you want to be proactive in getting your real estate license, it would be helpful. In most states, you will need to take courses that the state requires to sit for the salesperson license. Each state should have a home page for their Real Estate Commission's requirements for licensing. There are typically two types of license, a sales license and a broker's license. You have to have the sales license for a period of time, usually two years before you can take the exam for the broker's license. The difference in the two is that the broker's license allows you to open your own real estate company. You will need to find a broker to sponsor you and hold your sales license until you land at your new company.

Internships

If you're still in school, make it a top priority to secure an internship at a real estate company. This is a great way to confirm that the business is for you, and decide if you like the culture and environment at that firm.

It will also help you better understand the day-to-day roles and responsibilities of the different disciplines within the company. An internship will likely give you a leg up in getting hired by the company you intern with after you graduate. If you don't get hired full time by that firm, it will be a great addition to your resume as you begin interviewing.

If you are fortunate enough to get hired as an intern, make yourself as valuable as possible during your internship. Quickly learn what is expected of you and then find out how you can help the top producers with their projects. The people you are working for will know others in real estate and can be a great reference for you if you choose to work at another firm.

Interviewing

Once you get ready to pursue your career in real estate, you'll need a well written professional resume that touts your skills, education and experience. The goal in a resume is to accurately and positively relay your accomplishments to potential employers. Take credit for your contributions. Quantify your actions whenever appropriate. Your resume is the place to showcase your talents. Be sure to use specific details on tasks that you were in charge of and not just a standard job description. Include any pertinent accomplishments or successes that make you a top choice.

Most companies will want you to email your resume or complete an application online. Apply to ALL opportunities you are interested in and are qualified for. However, there's nothing better than writing a letter to the senior person in charge and hand delivering a copy to his or her office. It shows that you are serious about the job and it also gives you a sneak peek of the firm's space. You may even find a nugget of interest from the receptionist.

Interviewing for a job will give you your first taste of what the real estate business is all about. Try to secure as many interviews as possible. It is a terrific way to learn about the process itself and will also help you get more proficient at it. And, you'll learn more about the industry and the top producers.

Practice, practice and practice. Convey your passion about your goal of being in the real estate business. Prospective employers appreciate candidates who are driven and motivated. Don't be afraid to ask questions during your interview. In fact, you may want to create a list in advance. Ask about their training program, how compensation works during training and who you will be working with on a day-today basis. Your questions will take a little pressure off of you during your interview and will give you time to think about new questions to ask. Be sure to take notes; it shows you are interested and will allow you to address certain topics when you write your follow-up note to the interviewer.

Afterward, send a hand-written thank-you note or a typewritten signed letter – not an email or, even worse, a text message. Be brief, but be sure to mention things that particularly impressed you about the company/executive, and why you'd be a great hire.

A note of caution: be careful what you've posted on your Facebook page or other social media sites. You can be sure that prospective employers will be doing their online research, and one bad party picture could ruin your chances.

Mentors and Coaches

Finding a mentor or coach who will work with you to keep you focused, motivated and accountable as you pursue your professional goals will be important. Hopefully, your new employer will have a training program. If not, visit with as many senior members of the firm as you can and, again, do your research on them prior to meeting with them. Find out what their specialty is within the discipline, and learn about standout projects/achievements they have completed during their career. If it's something that's listed on their online bio or resume, you know it's something they're proud of and it will make a good conversation-starter.

If you join a firm where there is no training program and a company mentor is not available, consider hiring a third-party professional coach who specializes in real estate to work with you. Do your due diligence, and make sure he or she is well respected in the industry. Interview a handful of coaches and make sure you understand how they're compensated. Don't be afraid to ask for references from other clients, then make calls to those references to learn about their experiences and how the coaches have helped. Remember, this is your career we are talking about and you need to be very particular about who helps you shape your future.

CHAPTER 22

THE REAL WORLD

Every real estate professional has things they wish they had known when they first got into the business. Here are notes on some things that aren't necessarily taught in business school.

Professionalism

Commercial real estate is not just a job, it's a profession! There are two things you can control in your career: your time and your reputation. Be wise and thoughtful about how you want to be known and perceived within the industry. You are entering a business climate where potential employers and clients know a lot of people in the community. Remember that your reputation WILL proceed you. It is easy to be a great person when things are going well; how you handle the tough times will determine your character and your resolve. It is not easy! In some disciplines, like tenant representation or leasing, you may get told "no" a lot. Those who are persistent and stay after it day after day are the ones who will find long-term success.

Money

There are a number of ways in which real estate professionals in different disciplines are compensated. But here's one piece of advice that holds true in all cases: be smart about how you manage your money. You'll quickly learn that real estate is a cyclical business. There will be ups and downs. Just because you join a firm and are earning a salary doesn't necessarily mean you have it made. In a downturn, firms will cut back, and often, the last person in is the first person out. Save as much money as possible for the down cycles. My mentor told me to keep a year's living expenses in the bank at all times. There have been two times in my career where that advice kept me in business. This is not a doomsday forecast but a reality check for you. There is a lot of revenue potential in real estate, but you have to be prepared and cautious so that you can make it a career and not short-term hit-and-run attempt.

Ramp-Up

Success in real estate is rarely immediate. When you get into the business, you should plan on a two-to-three year ramp-up. Even if there is a training program at your new company, you will have to have the real-life lessons and time in the trenches to understand your role, responsibilities and how to advance within your discipline. Hopefully, it won't take the full two or three years, but you should be prepared that this could be the case. When you look at the time commitment over career that can span 30 years or more, it's not a bad investment of time and shorter than most stints in college.

Networking

Networking will be a big part of your real estate career. There are many ways to build relationships with others and create connections that can lead to business opportunities. Industry organizations (see Resources) provide a great opportunity for meeting established professionals who, more often than not, are willing to help make introductions or point you in the right direction as you begin your career. Many groups also have special "sub groups" especially for young professionals.

As you grow, you will establish relationships with clients and within your community whom you will be able to network. These relationships can be very valuable so treat them as such. You never know where future business will come from. However, as George Bush wrote in his book <u>41</u>, "There's a limit to the power of connections. While they can open doors, they cannot guarantee success".

Giving Back

One of the most important things you can do as a real estate professional is to give back to your profession and your community. By getting involved in industry organizations early in your career, you will be able to help those groups in fundraising, organizing their events or participating in various activities. Along the way, you will meet new people that you will likely do business with for years to come.

Besides having a good career strategy, giving back to your community is one of the most gratifying things you can do. You may have to volunteer for a number of groups before you find one that sparks your passion. But once you have found that organization, do everything you can to help them accomplish their mission. It took me working with five different charitable groups before I found the one for me. Mine is Camp John Marc, a camp for chronically ill children. All of the proceeds of this book will go to Camp John Marc, so thank you for helping the camp.

Another great way to give back is to become a mentor to yourself. Your career experience could be invaluable for the next generation of real estate professionals.

Commitment

Once you have determined that the commercial real estate business is for you, give it your all – 100 percent! Always do the right thing and don't cut corners. The shortcuts never pay off in the long run. Your hard work and attitude will determine your ultimate success.

Good luck and have fun in your new career!

Acknowledgements

This book could not have been possible without the help of some very special people. My mother the English teacher and my father the real estate executive motivated me to be the best I could be as a real estate professional. Rick Hughes helped me get my first job at Cushman and Wakefield. My mentor Tom Kelly taught me the importance of learning how to listen and be a professional. Christine Perez was the motivator behind the scenes. Many others contributed their professional expertise on their specific subject matter including David Snyder, Cindy Simpson, Jeff Turner, Rebecca Smith, Craig Wilson, Jack Crews, John St. Clair, James Ray, Kim Butler, Ali Greenwood, Curt Holcomb, Marijke Lantz, Toby Grove, Chris Harris, Mark Reeder, Vince Burt, Bill Cawley, Robert Shaw, Greg Fuller, Robert Jimenez, Marty Collins, Justin Keane, Dennis Barnes, Ray Mackey Jr, Brad Savage, Jeff Eckert, Walt Bialas, Sam Wood, Tim Jordan, Lauren Zimmer, Adam Saphire, Andrew Levy and Donna Weitzman.

Lee Ann Ridley was dynamite helping with the graphics and publishing. Harvey Mireles was terrific at editing and helping with publication.

Resources
(groups and organizations)

Below are groups and organizations that are a great resource for you to explore when considering a career in commercial real estate. Some groups have been previously mentioned in the book. All of the groups and organizations have a national conference and have local offices in the major markets of the US. Within the local markets, these groups welcome visitors to their offices and meetings. Call the local office and ask about attending a meeting or meeting with a staff member to learn more about the group and its networking benefits.

The American Institute of Architects (AIA) www.AIA.org

The Associated Contractors of America (AGC) www.AGC.org

Association for Computer Operations Management (AFCOM) www.AFCOM.com

National Multifamily Housing Council (NMHC) www.NMHC.org

Urban Land Institute (ULI) www.ULI.org

Society of Industrial and Office Realtors (SIOR) www.SIOR.com

International Council of Shopping Centers (ICSC) www.ICSC.org

National Association of Industrial and Office Parks (NAIOP) www.NAIOP.org

Certified Commercial Investment Member (CCIM) www.CCIM.com

Building Owners and Managers Association (BOMA) www.BOMA.org

Appraisal Institute www.appraisalinstitute.org

National Association of Realtors (NAR) www.NAR.Realtor/ Commercial

Institute of Real Estate Management (IREM) www.irem.org

Commercial Real Estate Women (CREW) www.crewnetwork.org

Most major markets will have a local Commercial Association of Realtors organization.